# Let's Explore
# Engineering

by Joe Levit

BUMBA BOOKS™

LERNER PUBLICATIONS ◆ MINNEAPOLIS

**Note to Educators:**

Throughout this book, you'll find critical-thinking questions. These can be used to engage young readers in thinking critically about the topic and in using the text and photos to do so.

Lerner Publications Company
A division of Lerner Publishing Group, Inc.
241 First Avenue North
Minneapolis, MN 55401 USA

For reading levels and more information, look up this title at www.lernerbooks.com.

**Library of Congress Cataloging-in-Publication Data**

Names: Levit, Joseph, author.
Title: Let's explore engineering / by Joe Levit.
Description: Minneapolis : Lerner Publications, [2019] | Series: Bumba books. A first look at STEM | Audience: Ages 4–7. | Audience: K to grade 3. | Includes bibliographical references and index.
Identifiers: LCCN 2017060847 (print) | LCCN 2017053542 (ebook) | ISBN 9781541507814 (eb pdf) | ISBN 9781541503274 (lb : alk. paper) | ISBN 9781541526990 (pb : alk. paper)
Subjects: LCSH: Engineering—Juvenile literature. | Engineers—Juvenile literature.
Classification: LCC TA149 (print) | LCC TA149 .L47 2019 (ebook) | DDC 620—dc23

LC record available at https://lccn.loc.gov/2017060847

Manufactured in the United States of America
1-43822-33655-1/23/2018

# Table of
# Contents

What Is Engineering? 4

Engineering Wonders 22

Picture Glossary 23

Read More 24

Index 24

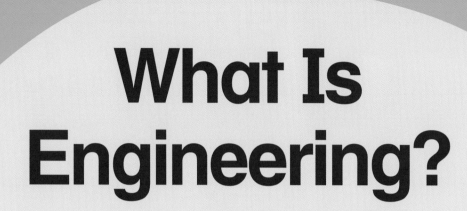

# What Is Engineering?

*Engineering* means "to plan

or build something."

Engineers use math

and science.

They create things that

solve problems.

There are many kinds
of engineers.

Some engineers help
build bridges.

A bridge has many parts
that fit together.

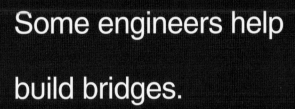

Why do people

build bridges?

Engineers think about designs

for a bridge.

Then they choose the design

that will work best.

Some engineers work with doctors.

They think about tools doctors can

use to help sick people.

Engineers also plan roads.
People use engineering to
make many different things.

Computer engineers work on

computer chips.

The chips run computers.

**What do people do on computers?**

Other engineers create machines for

outer space.

Engineers helped build the Mars rover.

It lets us explore the planet Mars.

Sports stadiums hold many fans.

People need to get in and out of

stadiums quickly.

Engineers create designs that will

help people move easily.

Think like an engineer.

Find a problem.

Then make a design to fix it!

21

# Engineering Wonders

Here are some things that engineers built.

What other objects do engineers work on?

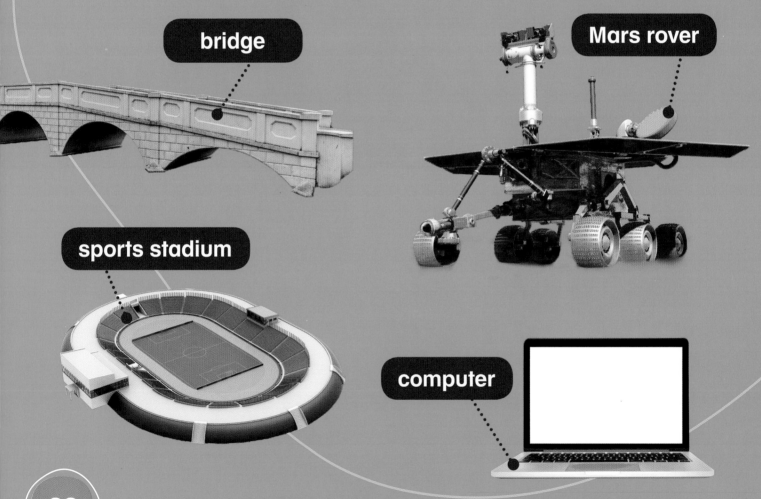

bridge

Mars rover

sports stadium

computer

# Picture Glossary

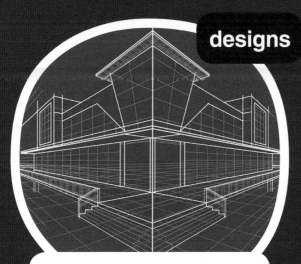

**designs**

plans written on paper or a computer

**engineers**

people who make designs to build things

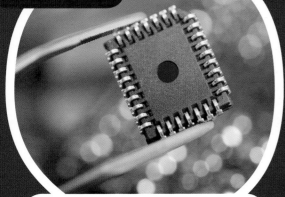

**computer chips**

computer parts that store information

**Mars rover**

a vehicle that explores the planet Mars

# Read More

Ball, Jacqueline A. *What Makes a Building Strong?* Egremont, MA: Red Chair, 2017.

Heos, Bridget. *Let's Meet a Construction Worker.* Minneapolis: Millbrook Press, 2013.

Ripley, Catherine. *Why? The Best Ever Question and Answer Book about Nature, Science and the World around You.* Berkeley, CA: Owlkids Books, 2018.

# Index

bridge, 7–8

computer, 15

doctor, 10

Mars, 16

problem, 4, 20

road, 13

stadium, 19

## Photo Credits

The images in this book are used with the permission of: icons: © Amy Salveson/Independent Picture Service; KN Studio/Shutterstock.com, p. 5; Luciano Mortula—LGM/Shutterstock.com, pp. 6–7; Hanyu Qiu/Shutterstock.com, p. 9; Rido/Shutterstock.com, p. 11; Stockr/Shutterstock.com, p. 12; kritsada doungdao/Shutterstock.com, p. 14; NASA/JPL, pp. 17, 22 (top right), 23 (bottom right); Leonard Zhukovsky/Shutterstock.com, p. 18; CroMary/Shutterstock.com, p. 21; Aurelian Nedelcu/Shutterstock.com, p. 22 (top left); 3DMAVR/Shutterstock.com, p. 22 (bottom left); Goran Bogicevic/Shutterstock.com, p. 22 (bottom right); stockshoppe/Shutterstock.com, p. 23 (top left); Monkey Business Images/Shutterstock.com, p. 23 (top right); Bluskystudio/Shutterstock.com, p. 23 (bottom left).

Front cover: Max Topchii/Shutterstock.com.